Beaded Bracelets

From the pages of *Bead&Button* magazine

KALMBACH
BOOKS

Printed in the United States of America

04 05 06 07 08 09 10 11 12 13   10 9 8 7 6 5 4 3 2 1

Visit our website at
http://kalmbachbooks.com
Secure online ordering available

Managing Art director: Lisa Bergman
Book layout: Kristine Brightman
Project editors: Julia Gerlach, Pam O'Connor
Photography: Bill Zuback, Jim Forbes

Acknowledgements: Stacy Blint, Mindy Brooks, Terri Field, Lora Groszkiewicz, Kellie Jaeger, Diane Jolie, Patti Keipe, Alice Korach, Tonya Limberg, Debbie Nishihara, Cheryl Phelan, Carrie Rohloff, Carole Ross, Candice St. Jacques, Maureen Schimmel, Lisa Schroeder, Terri Torbeck, Elizabeth Weber, Lesley Weiss

These designs are for your personal use. They are not intended for resale.
The projects in this booklet have appeared previously in *Bead&Button* magazine.

Contents

Great ideas and inspiration for all beaders!

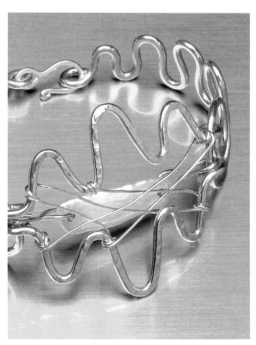

Basics

Conditioning thread

Conditioned thread doesn't tangle as readily as unconditioned thread. Conditioning straightens and strengthens thread and helps it resist fraying and separating. Use either beeswax (not candle wax or paraffin) or Thread Heaven to condition unwaxed beading thread like Nymo. Beeswax adds tackiness that is useful if you want your beadwork to fit tightly. Thread Heaven adds a static charge that causes the thread to repel itself, so it can't be used with doubled thread. All nylon threads (Nymo and Silamide, which is pre-waxed) stretch, so as part of conditioning, stretch the thread. Pull Nymo through beeswax or Thread Heaven after stretching it.

Knots

half-hitch knot

Come out a bead and form a loop perpendicular to the thread between beads. Bring the needle under the thread away from the loop. Then go back over the thread and through the loop. Pull gently so the knot doesn't tighten prematurely.

lark's head knot

A lark's head knot is commonly used to start macramé. Fold a cord in half and lay it behind a ring, loop, bar, etc. with the fold pointing down. Bring the ends through the ring from back to front then through the fold and tighten.

overhand knot

Make a loop in the cord and bring the end that crosses on top behind the loop. Then pull it through to the front.

pearl knotting

String a knotted necklace on doubled cord, starting with cord four times the desired finished length plus 8 in. (20cm). String a bead tip (if using them), all the beads, and the second bead tip. Push everything that will follow the first knot to the needle end of the cord.

1 Loop the cord around the first three or four fingers of your nondominant hand with the bead tip end on top.

2 Pinch the cross between your thumb and index finger. Hold the cord circle open on your spread fingers with your palm up. Then drop the bead end of the cord through the circle into your hand.

3 Put a long T-pin or an awl into the loop the same way the cord goes through. Gradually tighten the loop as it slips off your fingers, keeping the awl in it. Slide the awl toward the spot where you want the knot to be as you pull the bead end of the cord in the opposite direction. When the knot is right against the bead tip, let the cord slip off the tip of the awl. To set the knot, pull the two cord strands in opposite directions. Slide the next bead to the knot and repeat.

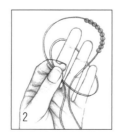 

square knot

1 Cross the left-hand cord over the right-hand cord, and then bring it under the right-hand cord from back to front. Pull it up in front so both ends are facing upwards.

2 Cross right over left, forming a loop, and go through the loop, again from back to front. Pull the ends to tighten the knot.

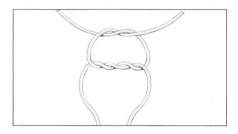

surgeon's knot

Cross the right end over the left end and go through the loop. Go over and through again. Cross the left end over the right end and go through once. Pull the ends to tighten.

Loops

wrapped loops

1 Make sure you have at least 1¼ in. (3.2cm) of wire above the bead. With the tip of your chainnose pliers, grasp the wire directly above the bead. Bend the wire above the pliers into a right angle.

2 Using roundnose pliers, position the jaws vertically in the bend.

3 Bring the wire over the top jaw of the roundnose pliers.

4 Keep the jaws vertical and reposition the pliers so the lower jaw fits snugly in the loop. Curve the wire downward around the bottom of the roundnose pliers. This is the first half of a wrapped loop.

5 Position the jaws of your chainnose pliers across the loop.

6 Wrap the wire around the wire stem, covering the stem between the loop and the top bead. Trim the excess wire and gently press the cut end close to the wraps with chainnose pliers.

plain loops

1 Trim the wire or head pin ⅜ in. (1cm) above the top bead. Make a right-angle bend close to the bead.

2 Grab the wire's tip with roundnose pliers. Roll the wire to form a half circle. Release the wire.

3 Position the pliers in the loop again and continue rolling, forming a centered circle above the bead.

4 The finished loop.

opening and closing

1 Hold the jump ring with two pairs of chainnose pliers or chainnose and roundnose pliers, as shown.

2 To open the jump ring, bring one pair of pliers toward you and push the other pair away.

 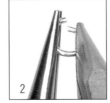

3 The open jump ring. Reverse the steps to close.

Flattened crimp

1 Hold the crimp using the tip of your chainnose pliers. Squeeze the pliers firmly to flatten the crimp. Tug the clasp to make sure the crimp has a solid grip on the wire. If the wire slides, repeat the steps with a new crimp.

2 Tug on the wires to make sure the flattened crimp is secure.

 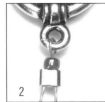

Folded crimp

1 Position the crimp in the notch closest to the crimping pliers' handle.

2 Separate the wires and firmly squeeze the crimp.

3 Move the crimp into the notch at the pliers' tip and hold the crimp as shown. Squeeze the crimp, folding it in half at the indentation.

4 Make sure the folded crimp is secure.

Off-loom bead-weaving stitches

bead ladder

1 A ladder of seed or bugle beads is most often used to begin brick stitch: Pick up two beads. Leave a 3-4-in. (8-10cm) tail and go through both beads again in the same direction. Pull the top bead down so the beads are side by side. The thread exits the bottom of bead #2. String bead #3 and go back through #2 from top to bottom. Come back up #3.

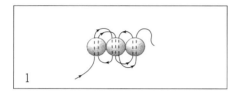

2 String bead #4. Go through #3 from bottom to top and #4 from top to bottom. Add odd-numbered beads like #3 and even-numbered beads like #4.

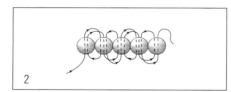

3 To stabilize the ladder, zigzag back through all the beads.

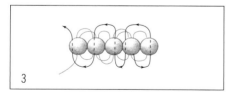

even-count flat peyote

1 String one bead and loop through it again in the same direction, leaving a 3-4-in. (8-10cm) tail. (Remove the extra loop and weave the tail into the work after a few rows.) String beads to total an even number. These beads comprise the first two rows.

2 Every other bead from figure **1** drops down half a space to form row 1. To begin row 3 (count rows diagonally), pick up a bead and stitch through the second bead from the end. Pick up a bead and go through the fourth bead from the end. Continue in this manner. End by going through the first bead strung.

3 To start row 4 and all other rows, pick up a bead and go through the last bead added on the previous row. To end a thread, weave through the work in a zigzag path, making a few half-hitch knots along the way. To resume stitching, begin a new thread the same way, exiting the last bead added in the same direction.

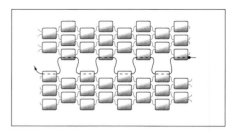

join peyote pieces

To join two sections or the beginning and end of a flat peyote piece invisibly, match up the two pieces so the "high" and "low" beads fit together. "Zip up" the pieces by going through each high and low bead, alternating pieces/ends.

right-angle weave

1 To start the first row, string four beads and tie into a snug circle with a square knot. Pass the needle through the first three beads again.

2 Pick up three beads (#5, 6, and 7) and sew back through the last bead of the previous circle (#3) and #5 and 6.

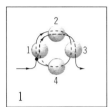

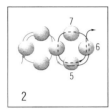

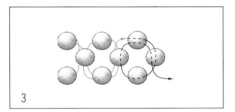

3 Pick up three beads and sew back through #6 and the first two new beads. Continue adding three beads for each stitch until the first row is the desired length. You are sewing circles in a figure-8 pattern and alternating direction with each stitch.

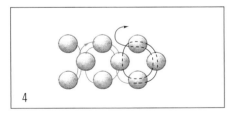

4 To begin row 2, sew through the last three beads of the last stitch on row 1, exiting the bead at the edge of one long side.

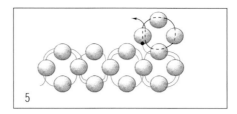

5 Pick up three beads and sew back through the bead you exited in figure **4** (the first "top" bead of row 1) and the first new bead, sewing in a clockwise direction.

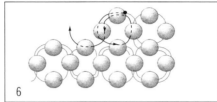

6 Pick up two beads and sew through the next top bead of the row below and the last bead of the previous stitch. Continue through the two new beads and the next top bead of the row below, sewing counter-clockwise. Keep the thread moving in a figure-8. Pick up two beads for the rest of the row. Don't sew straight lines between stitches.

square stitch

1 String the required number of beads for the first row. Then string the first bead of the second row and go through the last bead of the first row and the first bead of the second row in the same direction. The new bead sits on top of the old bead and the holes are horizontal.

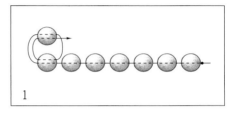

2 String the second bead of row 2 and go through the next-to-last bead of row 1. Continue through the new bead of row 2. Repeat this step for the entire row.

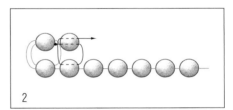

Easy strung bracelet

Beading doesn't get much easier than this. String together an assortment of pearls and crystals for a simply elegant double-strand bracelet that requires only one crimp bead in its assembly. You don't have to attach a clasp, tie a knot, or wrap any wire loops to make this beautiful, finished piece.

❶ Cut a 20-in. (51cm) strand of beading wire. Slide a 2mm spacer to the center of the wire and fold the wire in half. String the 12mm bead and four spacers over both wires (**photo a**).

❷ Slide one spacer onto each wire to separate the strands. String a pleasing mix of beads on each strand, placing a spacer after each one. String 6 in. (15cm) of beads for a 7-in. (18cm) bracelet. (Don't include the 12mm bead in your bracelet measurements.)

As you work, consider how the strands look individually as well as when the two are next to each other. Try to place larger beads next to smaller ones and crystals next to pearls to create an interesting, balanced design. Make any adjustments in length before continuing to the next step.

❸ Slide a spacer onto each wire, then string a crimp bead over both wires (**photo b**). String spacers over both wires until you have enough for a loop that will fit over the 12mm bead. Take the wires through the crimp again and continue through a few beads on each strand (**photo c**). Tighten the beads by gently pulling on the wires until no wire shows between beads. Leave enough ease to keep the bracelet flexible. Crimp the crimp bead (see "Basics," p. 4) and trim the excess wire. ❂ – *Irina Miech*

a

b

c

materials

- **50-60** assorted 3-8mm pearls and crystals
- **75-100** 2mm round sterling silver spacer beads
- 12mm bead for clasp
- 20-in. (51cm) flexible beading wire, .010 or .012
- sterling silver crimp bead

Tools: crimping or chainnose pliers
Optional: 10-15 assorted silver beads

Color-family bracelets

Multi-strand bracelets in a single color family appeal to people of all ages. Make them in seasonal colors or choose a hue that coordinates with a few of your favorite outfits.

Boost the visual appeal and stringing fun of these ten-strand bracelets by stringing some of the strands with simple, repeating patterns. Use Japanese seed beads if you can because they have larger holes than Czech seed beads.

❶ Measure your wrist circumference. An average-size bracelet takes 6¾-6⅞ in. (17-17.4cm) of beads.
❷ Without cutting the thread from the spool, string ten groups of beads, each the length determined in step 1. String one larger-holed bead (6º) at the end of each group.
❸ Slide the beads down the elastic until 8 in. (20cm) or more of unstretched thread shows at the needle end.

❹ Leaving about 6 in. (15cm) of elastic between the first and second group, cut off the first group. Pulling the elastic a little so there will be no slack, tie a surgeon's knot (see "Basics," p. 4)
❺ Thread one end through the last large-hole bead. Push the beads away from the knot then dot the knot with glue and pull it inside the large-hole bead (**inset photo**). Let dry before trimming.
❻ Complete the other nine bracelets.
❼ If you want to keep all ten of your bracelets together as a unit, you can make a small "bracelet" for your bracelet. String enough beads to wrap loosely around all ten strands and then secure it around the group of strands with a surgeon's knot. Let dry before trimming. **◉** – *Louise Malcolm*

materials
- variety of beads from one color family in some of these categories:
  - size 11º Japanese seed beads
  - size 8º seed beads
  - size 6º seed beads
  - **50-100** 3mm fire-polished beads
  - **50-100** 4mm fire-polished beads
  - **40-50** 4mm Swarovski crystals
  - **100** 3-4mm round Czech glass beads
  - **40-50** 6x4mm teardrops
- elastic sewing thread, white or black
- twisted wire beading needle
- G-S Hypo-tube Cement

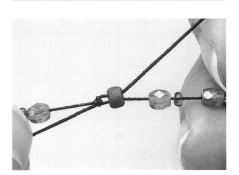

Power bead bracelet

Ethnic jewelry, characterized by chunky beads, natural textures, and earthy but vibrant colors, is tremendously popular. This bracelet—an adaptation of a Tibetan necklace—is comprised of carnelian, turquoise, freshwater pearls, and dZi beads. dZi beads date from 500-800 A.D. They are chemically etched banded and eyed agate beads. Traditionally, religious Tibetans consider them gods that have fallen to earth in the form of stones and believe the patterns are natural. The more valuable "pure dZi" are plumply rounded bicones with patterns of circles or eyes.

Fake dZi are widely available these days. Many come from China, which also produces some very good imitation etched carnelian that you can substitute for the dZi. You'll find them in bead stores and from many traders.

❶ Cut three lengths of nylon beading cord about five times the desired length of the bracelet. String a size 6° or 8° seed bead to the center of the three cords. Then pass all six ends through the clasp bead.

❷ Divide the cords into three pairs and braid them for about ⅛ in. (3mm). Tie an overhand knot (see "Basics," p. 4) against the braid.

❸ String one pearl on each pair of cords. You may have to put a needle on each cord and string the pairs of cords through the pearls one at a time. Knot the bundle of cords together against the pearls (**photo a** and see "Pearl knotting" in "Basics").

4 String all six ends through one of the stone beads and tie an overhand knot against it.

5 Then string two to four pearls on each pair of cords (**photo b**). Knot the bundle of cords against the pearls as shown in **photo a**.

6 Repeat steps 4 and 5, ending with step 4 and the last stone bead.

7 Repeat step 3, stringing one pearl on each cord pair.

8 Braid the three pairs of cords until the braid is long enough to make a loop that will fit securely over the clasp bead. Braid ½ in. (1.3cm) more. Fold the braid back to make the loop, bringing the tails to the end pearls (**photo c**).

9 Tie the loop with an overhand knot ⅛ in. from the pearls. Don't pull the knot tight yet. Make sure the loop fits over the clasp bead and will be snug when the knot has been tightened. You may have to braid a little more or unbraid a bit. When the loop is the right size, pull the knot tight (**photo d**).

10 String a pearl on each pair of cords. Secure each pearl with an overhand knot about ⅛ in. away from the pearl (**photo e**). Dot the knots with glue. Then cut the excess cord off, leaving ⅛-in. tails. ● – *Alice Korach*

a

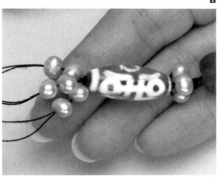

b

c

d

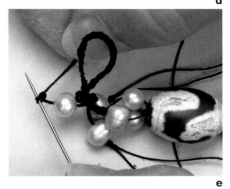

e

materials

- 16-in. (41cm) strand 4-6mm freshwater pearls
- **1-3** fake stone or glass dZi beads
- **1-3** dark red carnelians
- **1-3** greenish turquoise beads (these are small Tibetan turquoise beads)
- flat bead for a clasp
- size 6º or 8º seed bead that won't go through the clasp bead's hole
- nylon bead cord, size 1-3, or upholstery thread
- twisted wire needles
- G-S Hypo Cement
- **Tools:** awl

Fun fringed band

Use lots of beaded fringe to make exotic-looking bracelets. Start this project with a button or a beaded ball (directions at far right) and then string a single strand of beads, ending with a loop at the other end. The fun starts when you add three branches of fringe to each of the beads on the base strand.

the base

❶ Measure your wrist and add 1 in. (2.5cm) to allow for the closure and the shrinkage that occurs with the large number of fringes.

❷ To make the base, thread a needle with 1 yd. (.9m) of Nymo D. String a size 11º or larger seed bead to the middle of the thread. (If you're using a two-hole button, sew up through one hole, string three size 11º beads, and sew down through the other hole.) Then thread the second tail on the needle so you have a doubled thread with a bead or the button at the center.

❸ If you're using a beaded ball, string it on the doubled thread. Then string the base beads to just short of the measurement in step 1. The beaded ball or button is not part of this length.

❹ String enough beads for a loop that will just fit over your beaded ball or button and run the needle through the loop beads a second time for security.

❺ Go back through the last bead in the base row (**photo a**) and make a half-hitch knot (see "Basics," p. 4). Go through a few more beads, make another half-hitch knot, and repeat once or twice before cutting the thread.

the fringes

To make a thick bracelet like these, put a group of three fringes on every bead

in the base except the first and last two beads. If you prefer, make two fringes per bead. To help keep your thread from tangling in the fringes you've made, hold your nondominant hand around the fringed portion of the bracelet.

❶ Thread a needle on a length of Nymo you can handle. Working with a single thread, sew into the sixth bead from the ball toward the ball and tie a half-hitch knot. Go through the fifth bead and tie another half-hitch knot.

Then bring your thread out the third bead from the ball (**photo b**).

❷ Use your imagination as you go through all the seed beads, crystals, and small dangle beads you have been accumulating to choose your fringe beads. Vary the sizes and shapes of the beads for a more textural look. The bracelet fills out nicely if you use one to two size 11º seed beads at the base of the fringe and then put in a large bead or two.

❸ To begin a fringe group, string two

a

b

c

size 11º beads as shown in the **figure**. The first bead will be the connector or base for all three of the fringes in the group. String a combination of three to seven large and small beads for the stem of the fringe. Then string a group of large and small beads for a loop at the end of the fringe. Go back down the stem beads and the second 11º bead strung. String the second fringe like the first, and then string the third. Be sure to keep each fringe snug.

4 When you go back down the third fringe, continue through the connector bead at the base of the group. Go back through the base bead from the ball side and continue through the next base bead (**photo c**). Make another three-fringe group on top of this base bead.

5 Repeat steps 3-4, stopping two beads before the loop. End your thread as described in step 6.

6 To add thread, stop beading with at least 6 in. (15cm) of the old thread left. End this thread by running back up the stem of the last fringe, tying a half-hitch knot, going back down the stem, and making a half-hitch knot before the connector bead. Go up the stem of the middle fringe, knot, come back down, and knot as before. Run the thread up the stem of the first fringe and cut it off.

Tie on the new thread as you did in step 1, tying two or three half-hitch knot before exiting on the loop side of the first unfringed base bead. Resume fringing. ◗ – *Suzanne Golden*

materials

- 20-30g each assorted fringe beads of various sizes and shapes—size 6º to 15º seed beads, short bugles, cube beads, size 5º to 10º triangle beads, hex beads, tiny glass leaves or shapes, tiny tears, etc.
- 5g seed beads for base, either Japanese size 11ºs with large hole or size 10º or 8º seed beads
- beading needles, #10
- Nymo D beading thread
- beeswax or Thread Heaven
- beaded ball starting with an 8-10mm large-holed wooden bead; or use a 2-hole button

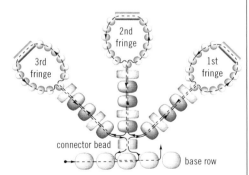

connector bead

base row

1st fringe

2nd fringe

3rd fringe

beaded ball

1 Thread 1 yd. (.9m) of Nymo through an 8-12mm large-hole bead and tie the thread tightly around the bead. Sew through the bead again to exit the hole.

2 String enough seed beads to reach around to the opposite side and sew back through the bead. Hold the bead at the holes to keep seed beads from getting inside.

3 Continue making spokes of beads around the big bead until seed beads meet around the holes (**photo d**).

4 String shorter lengths of beads between the spokes to fill in the gaps (**photo e**).

5 End the thread by going through beads on a spoke and tying at least three half-hitch knots. Cut the thread after going through a few beads. ◗

d

e

Leafy fringe bracelet

Make this fringe-embellished bracelet in bright colors for a wonderful springtime accessory. Or make it with silver beads to create a frosty, winter look. Feel free to get carried away with fringing. The icy silver bracelet on p. 14 has more fringe than called for in the directions below.

The embellishment on the bracelet is a leaf-shaped variation of branched fringe. A pattern for adding the fringe is provided, but there are no rules here. Add more or fewer, shorter or longer fringes to suit your style.

1 Measure your wrist and add 6 in. (15cm). Cut a piece of beading wire this length.

2 String half the clasp, a size 6º seed bead, a crimp bead, a size 6º seed bead, and a crimp bead on the wire to 2½ in. (6.3cm) from an end. Pass the end of the wire back through the beads and crimps (**photo a**). Tighten the loop around the clasp and crimp the crimp beads (see "Basics," p. 4).

3 String size 6º seed beads onto the wire and over the wire tail until it measures your wrist length plus ½ in. (1.3cm). String a crimp bead, a seed bead, a crimp bead, a seed bead, and the other half of the clasp. Thread the wire end back through the beads, exiting a few beads after the second crimp. Tighten the loop, leaving a little slack between the seed beads. Crimp the crimp beads. Trim any excess wire.

4 Thread a needle with 2 yd. (1.8m) of conditioned Nymo. String a size 15º seed bead to 2 in. (5cm) from the

a

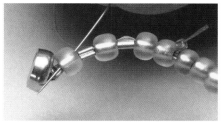

b

materials list
- 3g size 6º seed beads
- hank size 11º seed beads
- 3-4 size 15º beads to match size 6º beads
- 4 crimp beads
- magnetic clasp or your choice of clasp
- flexible beading wire, .019
- Nymo D beading thread
- beeswax or Thread Heaven
- beading needles, #10 or 12
- G-S Hypo Cement

Tools: chainnose or crimping pliers, diagonal wire cutters

Optional: 10-12 flower beads

thread's end and tie it with a surgeon's knot (see "Basics"). Glue the knot and allow it to dry. Trim the tail to ¼ in. (6mm). This is your "stop" bead. Repeat this step to start each new thread. End a thread by making and gluing several half-hitch knots (see "Basics") between the beads on a fringe.

5 Sew into the base four beads from the clasp, exiting the last bead before the clasp (**photo b**). The "stop" bead will be visible now but unnoticeable once the fringe is added.

6 String 15 size 11º seed beads to start a three-leaf fringe. Skip the last bead and sew back through the second-to-last bead. String seven beads. Count seven beads on the main strand from where the thread is exiting and sew through the eighth and ninth beads (**figure, a-b**).

7 String ten beads and sew back through the ninth bead (**figure b-c**). String seven beads and sew through the first bead strung for this leaf and up two more beads on the main strand (**figure c-d**).

8 Repeat step 6 to complete a three-leaf fringe and sew through the next size 6º

seed bead on the bracelet (**figure, d-e**).

9 String ten beads to make a single leaf fringe. Sew back through the second-to-last bead strung. String seven beads and sew back through first bead strung for this fringe. Sew through the next size 6º seed bead on the bracelet.

10 If adding flower beads, string a flower bead and a size 11º seed bead and sew back through the flower bead and up one size 6º bead on the bracelet.

11 Repeat steps 6-10 for the first 1½ in. (3.8cm) of the bracelet.

12 Begin to string 18 to 21 beads to make longer multiple-leaf fringes, adding four- or five-leaf branches on each one. Continue to add single-leaf fringes and flower beads between the branched fringes as desired.

13 Add four- and five-leaf fringes until 1½ in. remains on the bracelet. On the last 1½ in., alternate single-leaf and three-leaf fringes, ending with a three-leaf fringe in the space before the clasp.

14 End the thread as in step 4. ●

– *Ella Johnson-Bentley*

Wire and bead cuff

With a few turns of your roundnose pliers, you can easily create the coils and waves in this silver cuff. Shape the cuff's top section to frame a beautiful pearl or other special bead. Weave a fine-gauge wire through the top to keep your focal bead in place.

The bracelet consists of two side sections, a two-piece top section, and a focal bead wired into place.

Mrs J Warham
24 Redwood Avenue
Stone
Staffordshire
ST15 0DB

❶ Cut two 8-in. (20cm) and two 5-in. (13cm) pieces of 14-gauge wire.

❷ To make the bracelet's side sections, coil and bend the two longer pieces following the full-size template in **figure 1** or design your own pattern of loops and coils. Make sure to leave about ½ in. (1.3cm) of wire on each piece for a loop.

❸ Bend the two shorter wires following the template in **figure 2**. Again, modify the design as you like, but leave ½ in. of wire on each end of each piece to make the connecting loops. Plan the bracelet's top section

figure 1

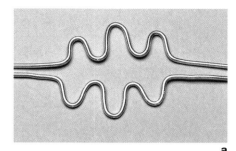

a

b

figure 2

figure 3

c

d

e

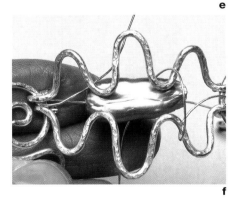

f

materials

- 3 ft. (.9m) 14-gauge sterling silver wire
- 1 ft. 24-gauge sterling silver wire, dead soft
- 2 in. (5cm) 18-gauge sterling silver wire, dead soft
- flat, oblong pearl or other bead, 25mm or longer, drilled through its length or on each end
- rouge cloth or silver polish

Tools: roundnose and chainnose pliers, hammer, wire cutters

Optional: bracelet mandrel

that fits comfortably around your wrist.

❾ String the pearl to the center of the 24-gauge wire. Center it behind the top section pieces and wrap the wire loosely around each side section coil, working between the two top section loops. Once the pearl is held in place, wrap the wire across it and through the curves of the top section pieces several times (**photo f**). When you're satisfied with the look, wrap each end of the 24-gauge wire around the 14-gauge wire and trim the excess.

❿ Use about 1¼ in. (3cm) of 18-gauge wire to make a hook for the clasp. Follow the template in **figure 3**, and then hammer both sides of the hook. Open the clasp loop and attach it to a loop on either side section. Close the loop.

⓫ Follow the product directions for using rouge cloth or silver polish to give the wire a lustrous finish. ●

– Wendy Witchner

to accommodate the wire wraps that surround the bead.

❹ Arrange the wire so the pieces are the mirror image of each other (**photos a** and **b**). Hammer the front surface of each piece to add strength and texture to the silver.

❺ Turn a ¼-in.- (6mm) diameter loop on each end of the top section pieces. Bend these loops toward the back and perpendicular to the rest of the piece (**photo c**). Cut off any excess wire.

❻ Turn a ¼-in. loop on the straight (back) end of each side section and cut off any excess wire (**photo d**). These should also be turned toward

the back and perpendicular to the piece.

❼ Open each loop on the top sections with a slight twist (never stress the loop by pulling back on it). Connect the top sections to the sides (**photo e**). Close the loops.

❽ Lay the bracelet over your wrist or a bracelet mandrel. Using your fingers, curve the hammered wire into a cuff

Afghani wire bangle

Traditional Middle Eastern wirework served as inspiration for this ethnic bracelet. Wire-coiled wire units are separated by lampwork glass beads by Beth Boal that resemble banded agate.

The directions below are for a 6½-in. (16.5cm) wrist. The inside circumference of the bangle is approximately 7 in. (18cm). Before you start, loosely measure your wrist with a soft tape measure. To adjust the size of the bangle, simply subtract 6½ in. from your wrist measurement and divide the difference by 4. Add that amount (to increase the size) or subtract (to decrease the size) for each of the 1 in. (2.5cm) coils in step 1 of "assembling the bracelet."

making the coils

Each coiled piece is constructed by wrapping a piece of wire around another wire. The straight wire core is used as a mandrel.

❶ Cut a 4½-ft. (1.4m) length of 18-gauge wire and bend it in half.

❷ Place the 12-gauge wire against the bend in the 18-gauge wire and hold it in place with your left hand. With your right hand, wrap the 18-gauge wire around the straight 12-gauge wire (**photo a**).

❸ When you reach the end of the first half of the 18-gauge wire, turn the piece around and wrap the other half. Set it aside.

❹ Cut a 3-in. (7.6cm) length of 18-gauge wire and bend it in half. Repeat steps 2-3 using the 14-gauge wire as the core. Set it aside.

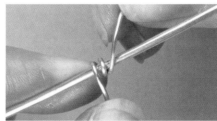

a

b

❺ Cut a 4-ft. (1.2m) length of 18-gauge wire and bend it in half. Repeat steps 2-3 using the 16-gauge wire as the core.

❻ Cut a 2-in. (5cm) length of 16-gauge wire and make a loop at one end (see "Basics," p. 4). The loop needs to be large enough to fit over 12-gauge wire.

❼ Remove the coil from the 16-gauge wire mandrel and cut a 1-in. length of coil (**photo b**).

❽ Slide the 1-in. coil over the wire and up against the loop. Make a second loop at the other end that is in the same plane as the first loop (**photo c**).

❾ Hold one loop in each hand between your thumb and index finger and gently bend the sides of the coil down around your thumbs (**photo d**)

to create a slight curve in the center.

❿ Use flatnose pliers to bend each loop perpendicular to the coiled center (**photo e**). The loops will be parallel to each other.

⓫ Repeat steps 5-10 until you have four curved coil components. Each one will be adjusted when the bracelet is assembled, so don't worry if the curves vary slightly.

making the clasp

❶ Remove the coil from the 14-gauge wire and cut a ¼-in. (6mm) long piece.

❷ Use the tip of the roundnose pliers to make a small loop (see "Basics") at one end of the 14-gauge wire.

❸ Grasp the wire with the largest part of the roundnose pliers next to the

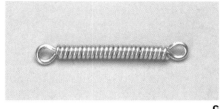

c

g

figure 1

figure 2

d

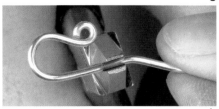

h

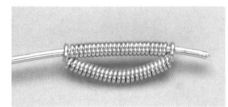

k

e

i

l

f

j

small loop at the end of the wire (**photo f**). With your thumb push the long wire around one jaw of the pliers until it is parallel to the loop (**photo g**).

❹ Use flatnose pliers to grasp the straight wire across from the small loop and make a slight bend in the wire away from the loop with your fingers (**photo h**). Refer to the template in **figure 1** and make necessary adjustments.

❺ Slide the ¼-in. coil from step 1 on the 14-gauge wire and push it up to the bend (**photo i**). Following the template in **figure 1**, make a loop at the end of the wire with roundnose pliers.

❻ Place the clasp component on the anvil and gently flatten the hook and loop with a hammer (**photo j**).

assembling the bracelet

❶ Remove the coil from the 12-gauge wire and cut four 1-in. coils.

❷ Following the template in **figure 2**, use the large part of the roundnose pliers to make a loop at one end of the 12-gauge wire.

❸ String a spacer, a lampwork bead, and a spacer on the wire. Slide the end of the wire through a loop on a curved coil piece, a 1-in. coil, and the other loop on the curved coil piece (**photo k**). You may need to adjust the curved coil slightly so the loops are lined up against the 1-in. coil.

❹ Repeat step 3 for each curved and 1-in. coil piece. End with a spacer, a lampwork bead, and a spacer.

❺ Make a loop next to the last spacer to match the first loop. Keep the loops in the same plane.

❻ Place a loop on the anvil and flatten it gently with a hammer. Repeat with the loop at the other end of the bracelet.

❼ With your hands, gently begin to

materials

- 10-12 in. (25-31cm) 12-gauge sterling silver wire
- 4 in. (10cm) 14-gauge sterling silver wire, dead soft
- 9 in. (23cm) 16-gauge sterling silver wire, dead soft
- 12 ft. (3.7m) 18-gauge sterling silver wire, dead soft
- **5** lampwork beads* (approx. 10mm diam.)
- **10** sterling silver spacers*

Tools: chainnose, flatnose, and roundnose pliers, wire cutters, hammer, anvil or bench block, tape measure
Bead holes must be large enough to fit over 12-gauge wire

form the bracelet into a round shape. Use flatnose pliers to adjust the loops on the curved coils (**photo l**) as you shape the bracelet.

❽ Open the loop (see "Basics") on the clasp. Slide the opened loop through a loop at the end of the bracelet and close the loop. ❍ – *Lori Merel*

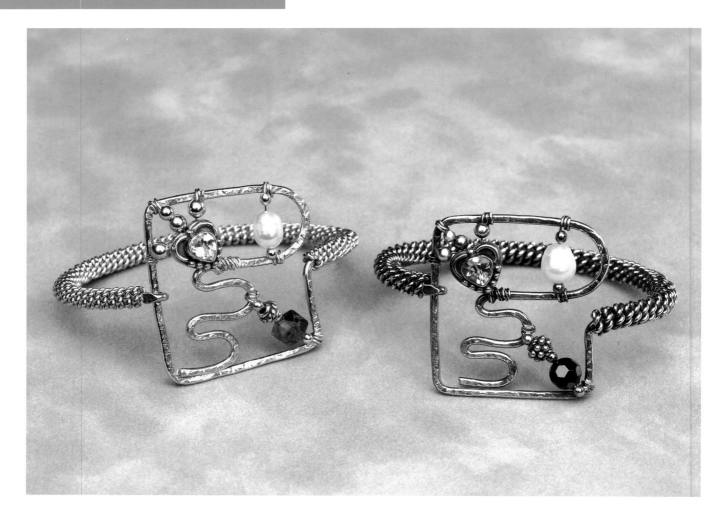

Embellished wire bracelet

Make an interesting centerpiece for a wire bracelet with an asymmetrical square, some decorative curves, and a few bead accents. Don't stop after making just one of these bracelets; play with the elements and come up with variations of your own.

1 Measure your wrist, allowing ½ in. (1.3cm) of ease. Cut a piece of 14-gauge wire 9 in. (23cm) longer than this measurement. Make a right-angle bend in the wire at your wrist-plus-ease measurement.

2 Bend the twisted wire in half, place the fold against the shorter side of the bent 14-gauge wire, and coil the twisted wire tightly around the core (**photo a**). When the coil is an inch (2.5cm) shorter than the core, slide it off and set it aside.

3 Shape the 9-in. section of wire into a decorative square. Follow the template in the **figure** above or design a centerpiece of your own.

4 Hammer the square to harden and add texture to the wire (**photo b**).

5 Cut five 3-in. (7.6cm) lengths of 24-gauge wire. Hold one piece of wire against the square where you want to place the first beads. (Refer to the photo above for all bead placement or vary the design as you like.) Allow ½ in. (1.3cm) of wire to extend beyond the square. Wrap the short end of the thinner wire around the thicker wire several times (**photo c**). Keep the wraps tight and close together. Dab a small amount of glue on the thicker wire to keep the coils in place, if necessary. Cut off the excess wire tail.

6 String a 2mm bead, a pearl, and a

a

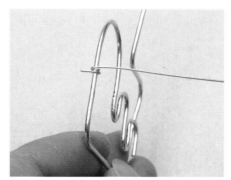

c

b

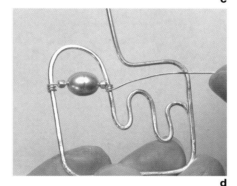

d

e

materials

- 20 in. (51cm) 14-gauge gold-filled or sterling silver wire
- 6 ft. (1.8m) 20-gauge gold-filled or sterling silver twisted wire
- 2 ft. (61cm) 24-gauge gold-filled or sterling silver wire, dead-soft
- **6** 2mm gold-filled or sterling silver beads
- **3** 3mm gold-filled or sterling silver beads
- 10mm freshwater pearl
- 8mm gemstone or crystal
- 3-4mm gold-filled or sterling silver Bali-style bead
- 3-hole heart-shaped charm

Tools: roundnose and chainnose pliers, wire cutters, hammer, anvil or steel block

Optional: cyanoacrylate glue

2mm bead on the wire you just attached. Coil the wire around another section of the square (**photo d**). Attach the crystal with 2mm beads and the Bali-style bead in the same way.

7 To string the heart charm or a substitute bead, attach three wires to a corner of the square as before. String a 3mm bead on each outer wire and a 2mm and 3mm bead on the center wire. (The small beads cover the wire between the square and the charm. Use more or fewer depending on your choice of charm or bead.) String the charm on all three wires and coil the ends around the center section of the square, as shown. Use chainnose pliers,

if necessary to wrap the wires. Trim the excess wire and squeeze the cut ends tightly against the square.

8 Slide the coil made in step 2 back on the 14-gauge core. Shape the wire around your wrist to determine the correct length for the bracelet. If the coil is too long, slide it off the core, trim it to the correct size, and replace it on the core. Trim the core wire, leaving about ½ in. extending beyond the coil.

9 When the coil-covered section is the right size, flatten the core's tip with a hammer. Use roundnose pliers to turn a small hook at the end of the core wire (**photo e**). ● – *Wendy Witchner*

Basic peyote bangle

The secret behind this gorgeous peyote bangle that keeps its shape no matter how many times you wear it is the memory wire hidden in its core. Once you've made this basic bangle, consider adding a little embellishment such as a pattern, fringing, or different bead sizes to liven things up.

Use a fray-resistant beading thread, such as Fireline, to stitch the peyote band. Keep your stitching fairly loose while making this bracelet or the band will buckle when you try to shape it into a tube. If you've never tried peyote stitch before, you may want to stitch a practice panel to get accustomed to the weave's pattern.

stitching the peyote band

❶ String a stop bead on a 2-yd. (1.8m) length of beading thread and go through it again in the same direction. String 7 in. (18cm) of hex-cut beads. Since it's easier to work in even-count than odd-count peyote, add or remove a bead, if necessary.

❷ Work in even-count peyote for 12 rows (see "Basics," p. 4). Pick through the hex cuts as you work, choosing beads of consistent size and even edges. If you have less than 2 ft. (61cm) of thread remaining once you've finished stitching, secure it in the beadwork and start a new 2-ft. length of thread.

❸ Cut or break off a 10-in. (25cm) piece of memory wire. To break the

wire, hold it with chainnose pliers and bend it back and forth at one point until it weakens and snaps off. Or use heavy-duty household wire cutters. Never cut memory wire with jewelry-weight wire cutters because you'll ruin them.

❹ Wrap the peyote band around the memory wire and sew through the bead on the opposite end of the edge row to begin "zipping up" the seam (see "Basics" and **photo a**). Sew through these two beads again to reinforce the stitching. String a bead on the memory wire and slide it into the center of the tube you just created (**photo b**). A hex-cut bead will fit perfectly into the tube's six-sided opening. Stitch through

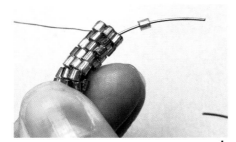

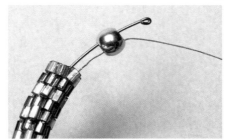

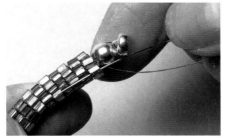

materials

- 20g size 8º seed beads, hex cuts
- 10 in. (25cm) bracelet-diameter memory wire
- 2 8mm large-hole metal beads or other cylindrical findings
- magnetic clasp
- fray-resistant beading thread or Fireline fishing line, 6 lb. test
- beading needles, #10

Tools: chainnose pliers, heavy-duty wire cutters

Optional: 2 3mm small-hole metal beads

the new bead and back through the bead your thread is exiting to hold it in place.

❺ Continue zipping up the seam and stringing beads on the memory wire to fill the tube (**photo c**). You don't need to stitch the filler beads to the tube until you reach the last row. Then stitch the filler bead in place as in step 4 to reinforce the tube's ends. Make sure you don't allow the tube to slip off the memory wire as you work.

finishing the ends

❶ Turn a small, U-shaped loop on the tip of the memory wire, working at the end of the bracelet where your thread exits. Use chainnose pliers to squeeze the loop until it is narrow enough to slide through the large-hole bead (**photo d**). Squeeze gently so the wire doesn't break. String a large-hole bead over the loop.

❷ Sew through the bead with your working thread (**photo e**). (You can also add a second, smaller bead as shown on the red bracelet on p. 22.) String half of the magnetic clasp, go back through the metal bead or beads, and sew into a hex cut on the end row of peyote (**photo f**). Tighten the thread so the clasp sits firmly in place next to the large-hole bead. Go back through an adjoining hex cut in the end row (working toward the clasp) and continue through the large-hole bead (or beads) and clasp loop as before. Turn and work back toward the tube. Repeat this step until you've gone through each bead on the end row. Bury the thread tail in the beadwork.

❸ Anchor 2 ft. of thread with half-hitch knots (see "Basics") at the other end of the bracelet. Before you attach the clasp at this end, try on the bracelet. Although you can't reduce the bracelet's

size, you can increase it if you need to. Work additional rows onto the edge row of peyote using brick stitch (see "Basics"). It will look the same as the peyote. Fill the additional length of the tube with beads as before. Stitch a hex cut in the center of the end row to finish the tube as in step 5 of "stitching the peyote band," above.

❹ When the bracelet is the right size, cut or break off the excess memory wire about ¼ in. (6mm) past the edge row of beads and turn a very small loop. (Because you have such a short piece of wire to work with, this end is slightly more difficult to complete.) Once you've turned the loop, finish this end to match the first.

❺ If the memory wire core is stiff, it can work against the magnetic clasps and pull them apart. To counter this, simply curve the ends gently inward with your fingers. With a little coaxing, you can easily bend the core wire so the bracelet takes on a completely round shape. ● – *Mindy Brooks*

Bugle bracelet

Antique and costume jewelry can be a great source of inspiration for your jewelry creations. This bracelet is an adaptation of an 1800s Victorian mesh bracelet made with tiny gold tubes and rondelles. In this inexpensive alternative, bugles and seed beads recreate the look. The band is stunning in one or multiple colors.

These directions are for the bracelets shown above. As an alternative, replace each bugle with five size 11° seed beads (**photo a**). All other instructions remain the same.

band

❶ Cut a 2-yd. (1.8m) length of beading thread and string a stop bead 8 in. (20cm) from the end. Go through the bead again in the same direction.
❷ String two seed beads, one bugle, two seeds, one bugle, and two seeds (**figure 1**). These beads form rows 1 and 2. To begin row 3, pick up a seed bead and go through the second-from-last seed bead in the opposite direction. Pick up a bugle and go through the next seed bead. Pick up a seed bead and go through the next bugle (**figure 2**). Work in flat, even-count peyote (see "Basics," p. 4).
❸ Continue adding rows until you reach the desired length of the bracelet, minus the length of the clasp. On the last completed row, the needle should exit the last seed at the top of the band.

a

b

e

c

f

d

clasp options

To attach a clasp, you'll need to add a few beads to the end rows of the band. The type of clasp will determine where beads need to be added. The instructions below refer to the clasps shown at left. Remove the stop bead before you begin.

rectangular box clasp (center bracelet)

❶ String a seed bead and go through the top loop of the clasp and the next seed bead (**photo b**).
❷ Go through the bugle and the next seed. Pass through the second loop on the clasp, string a seed bead, and go through the next bugle. String a seed bead, and go through the last loop on the clasp and the last seed bead. The bugles are inset a row.
❸ Go up through the seed bead to the left and retrace the thread path of the previous row. The needle will exit the last seed bead at the top of the band.
❹ Retrace the thread path (steps 1-3) several times to secure the clasp.
❺ Tie off the thread by weaving it back through the band and tie half-hitch knots (see "Basics") every once in a while. Trim the tail after going through a bead.
❻ Repeat on the other end.

magnetic clasp (bottom bracelet)

❶ Work one more row of peyote, but don't add a seed bead after the second bugle. Instead, pass the thread through the last two seed beads. The end seed bead on the top and bottom edge of the band should be sticking out slightly.
❷ Go up through the seed to the left

and back out the seed next to the last bugle (**photo c**).
❸ Pass the needle through the loop on the magnetic clasp and go through the seed bead again in the same direction (**photo d**). Repeat four or five more times to reinforce the clasp.
❹ Weave the thread up through the beads so the needle exits the last seed on the top edge of the band and repeat steps 2 and 3.
❺ Tie off the thread and trim the tail.
❻ Repeat on the other end.

slide clasp (top bracelet)

❶ Work another row of peyote, but don't add a seed bead after the first bugle. Instead, go through both middle seed beads and the next bugle. String a seed bead and exit the last seed bead.
❷ Slide the end of the band through a bar on the clasp (**photo e**).
❸ Fold the band over the bar. Close

figure 1

figure 2

materials

- 9g size 3 (2x7mm) bugle beads or 12g size 11º seed beads
- 7g size 11º seed beads
- 23mm filigree rectangular box clasp, slide clasp with 27mm bar, or **2** magnetic clasps
- beading needles, size #12
- Nymo D beading thread or Fireline fishing line, 6 lb. test
- beeswax or Thread Heaven for Nymo

up the fold by sewing back and forth between the beads on the end row and the row on the band where the two meet (**photo f**).
❹ Tie off the thread and trim the tail.
❺ Repeat on the other end. ◗
– *Gail Tanner*

Netted peyote band

Beads are an exciting medium for creating jewelry. Not only is there a vast array of material to choose from, but there also exists a wide range of patterns and stitches to use. On their own, these stitches are wonderful, but they can also be combined for even more variations. Here, peyote-stitched bugles and Japanese cylinder beads form the base of this lacy band. Rows of netting fill out the design, and a row of crystals embellishes the top.

The instructions that follow are for making the bracelets pictured above, but they're easy to modify. Try beads of other colors and sizes in the ruffles along the outer edges (steps 7 and 8). Make a thinner bracelet by stopping at

step 6. As you add crystals in step 9, skip every other opening. Or, use pearls in place of the crystals. As a word of caution, make sure you use a tough thread like Fireline if you want to pass directly through the loops of a magnetic clasp. The sharp edges will cut through most beading materials.

❶ Fold a 3-yd. (2.7m) length of thread in half and attach it to a clasp with a lark's head knot (see "Basics," p. 4). (You'll have two strands of equal length.) Thread a needle on one strand and string one crystal, three cylinder beads, and one bugle. Then string a repeating pattern of one cylinder bead and one bugle (**figure 1**) until the

bracelet is about equal to your wrist measurement. String three cylinder beads, one crystal, and the second half of the clasp. Check the fit again and make any necessary adjustments. Then go back through the crystal.

❷ Thread the needle onto the other strand. (Work with this strand until you have 8-12 in./20-30cm left at the end of a step, then switch to the other strand.) Go through the crystal and two cylinder beads. Pick up a cylinder and go through the next bugle. Continue in flat peyote (see "Basics") across the row (**figure 2**) until you reach the last two cylinder beads. Go through these beads and the crystal. Pin the bracelet to your work surface to make it easier to

a

b

figure 1

figure 2

figure 3

figure 4

figure 5

figure 6

figure 7

handle, if desired. Adjust the tension (not too tight) and slide the beads into place before continuing.

❸ Start the bracelet's inside lace section by going through the clasp, crystal, and three cylinder beads. *Pick up three cylinders and go through the next cylinder on the previous row.* Repeat from * to * (**figure 3**) until you reach the last three cylinder beads. Go through these cylinders and the crystal. The bracelet will curl slightly as you work.

❹ Go through the clasp and back through the crystal. Pick up four cylinder beads and go through the middle cylinder of the last three-bead group added in the previous row. *Pick up three cylinders and go through the middle bead of the next three-bead group.* Repeat from * to * (**figure 4**) until you've gone through the middle bead of the end three-bead set. Pick up four cylinders and go through the crystal.

❺ Go through the clasp, crystal, and three cylinder beads in the previous row. *Pick up a bugle and go through the middle cylinder in the previous row.* Repeat from * to * (**figure 5**) until you reach the last three cylinders. Go through the cylinders and crystal. Adjust the tension on this step so the bracelet is flat and straight.

❻ Go through the clasp, crystal, and two cylinder beads. *Pick up a cylinder and go through the next bugle.* Repeat from * to * (**figure 6**) until you reach the last three cylinder beads. Pick up a cylinder and go through the next two cylinders, but not the crystal.

❼ To start the ruffles, go through the

first three cylinders on the outer row opposite the row you just made. *Pick up three beads (change the color or size, if desired—smaller beads make a smoother edge) and go through a cylinder.* Repeat from * to * (**figure 7**) until you reach the last three cylinders. Go through the cylinders, but not the crystal.

❽ Repeat step 7 on the outer row of the opposite side of the bracelet. End by going through the crystal, clasp, and back through the crystal.

❾ To add the crystal embellishment, *pick up a 3mm crystal and go through the cylinder bead that connects the netting in the center of the bracelet (**photo a**).* Repeat from * to * until you reach the crystal next to the clasp. Go through the crystal, clasp, and back through the crystal, as before. Keep the tension tight to hold the crystals securely in place.

❿ If both strands are now at the same end of the bracelet, work each one through several beads, making half-hitch knots (see "Basics") between beads. If the strands are at opposite ends of the bracelet, you have two choices: Finish them as described above or try this alternate approach. Work each strand toward the bracelet's mid-point by going through crystals and cylinder beads as in step 9. When the strands meet, secure them with a surgeon's knot (see "Basics" and **photo b**), glue the knot, and hide it in a neighboring bead. Work the threads through a few beads and trim the tails. ❂ – *June Huber*

materials

- 7g size 11º Japanese cylinder beads
- 7g 3mm bugle beads
- **50** 3mm fire-polished beads
- toggle or magnetic clasp
- Nymo B or Silamide beading thread or Fireline fishing line, 6 lb. test
- beeswax or Thread Heaven for Nymo
- beading needles, #10 or 12

Optional: size 11º or 14º Japanese cylinder beads or seed beads (accent color)

Cable and channel bracelets

These sleek, classic bracelets designed by Beverly Mayfield, owner of the General Bead Store in San Francisco, demonstrate an interesting angle on peyote stitch. Instead of a flat piece or a hollow tube, the stitching forms a solid cable of beads which is then treated in one of two ways. Requiring just a few materials, the bracelets are versatile and easy to make. Go ahead and make several—they'll look great stacked up on your wrist.

Beverly created two versions of this design: the cable bracelet (the olive, copper, and purple bracelets in the photo above) and the channel bracelet (the teal/pink and blue/pink bracelets). The cable bracelet has size 11º seed beads strung between the 3.3 cylinder beads. The channel bracelet is made with two colors of cylinder beads. Size 8º hex-cut or twisted hex-cut beads can be substituted for the 3.3 beads.

cable bracelet

These directions make a bracelet 6¾ in. (17cm) long without a clasp; however, test the length after you string the first row of beads because 3.3 cylinder beads vary in length. The first row strung should be a multiple of four plus one additional bead. If you need to adjust the size of the bracelet, add or subtract four beads at a time.

❶ Start with 2 yd. (1.8m) of thread. Attach split rings to both sides of the magnetic clasp. (If you are using a lobster claw clasp, consider the loop on the claw end as a split ring in the directions.) Tie one end of the thread to a split ring on the clasp with a square knot (see "Basics," p. 4), leaving a 4-in. (10cm) tail. Glue the knot but don't cut the tail. Thread a needle on the working thread.

❷ String 65 3.3 cylinder beads. Check your bead count before proceeding.

❸ Sew through the split ring at the other end of the clasp and back through one bead. Leave a little slack in the strand because the bracelet will tighten up as you stitch.

❹ Connect the ends of the clasp so you can stitch the bracelet in a circle. If you weave it flat, it may be too stiff to bend into a circle afterwards. Work flat peyote stitch (see "Basics") across the row (**photo a**).

❺ Sew through the last bead in the row, the split ring, and back through the last bead again. Stitch across the row again, adding a third bead in the space where two beads are next to each other (**photo b**).

❻ At the end of the row, sew through the last bead, the split ring, and back through the last bead and one bead of first three-bead group. Pick up two size 11º seed beads and sew through the same bead in the second three-bead group. Sew through the next single bead on the

a

b

c

d

e

figure 1

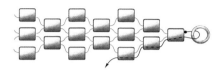

figure 2

materials

both projects

- magnetic or lobster claw clasp
- 2 split rings (1 if using a lobster claw)
- beading needles, #10
- Nymo D or Conso E (#69) beading thread in coordinating color
- beeswax or Thread Heaven
- G-S Hypo Cement or clear nail polish

cable bracelet

- **129** 3.3 Japanese cylinder beads or size 8º hex-cut beads
- **144** size 11º Japanese seed beads

channel bracelet

- **149** 3.3 Japanese cylinder beads or size 8º hex-cut beads, main color (MC)
- **29** 3.3 Japanese cylinder beads or size 8º hex-cut beads, accent color (AC)

half-hitch knot (see "Basics") between the beads. Sew through two beads and tie another half-hitch knot. Sew through a few more beads. Glue the knots and trim the tail. Thread a needle on the original 4-in. tail and sew through a few beads before trimming.

channel bracelet

These directions make a 6½-in. (16.5cm) bracelet, not including the clasp. If you need to shorten or lengthen the bracelet, add or subtract in multiples of two beads.

1 Repeat steps 1-4 of the cable bracelet. Start with 7 ft. (2.3m) of thread and string 61 main color beads. It is important not to let your stitches twist. Place the bracelet around a cardboard tube to prevent the beads from shifting.

2 When you've stitched one row, sew through the last bead, the split ring, and back through two beads to the other side of the first row and work another row of peyote stitch down the other edge of the bracelet (**figure 1**).

3 At the other end, sew through the last bead, the split ring, and back though three beads (**figure 2**).

4 String an accent color (AC) 3.3 cylinder bead and sew through the last bead sewn through in the same direction. Sew back through the AC bead again and flip the bead into the center of the bracelet.

5 Sew through the bead on the opposite edge of the bracelet (**photo d**). Sew back through the AC bead (**photo e**). Sew through the bead on the edge again and tighten the thread so that the peyote rows curve into a channel around the AC bead. Sew up two beads on the edge of the bracelet.

6 Repeat steps 4-5, adding AC cylinder beads until you reach the other end of the bracelet.

7 Finish as in step 8 of the cable bracelet. ◗ – *design by Beverly Mayfield, instructions by Carol Perrenoud*

groups, working in a straight line. Sew through the split ring and repeat the pattern, adding two seed beads in the third space of the same three-bead groups. To shape the bracelet into a curve, place fatter size 11º seed beads between the beads on the outer side of the bracelet and thinner size 11º seed beads between the beads on the inner side. Stitch snugly so that the bracelets have a stiff, bangle-like profile when worn.

8 At the end of the row, sew through the last bead, around the split ring, back through the last bead, and tie a

bracelet and the same bead of the third three-bead group. Pick up two size 11º seed beads and sew through the same bead in the fourth three-bead group (**photo c**). Continue adding two seed beads in every other opening between the three-bead groups along a straight line.

7 At the end of the row, repeat step 6, adding two seed beads in the spaces between beads of the same three-bead

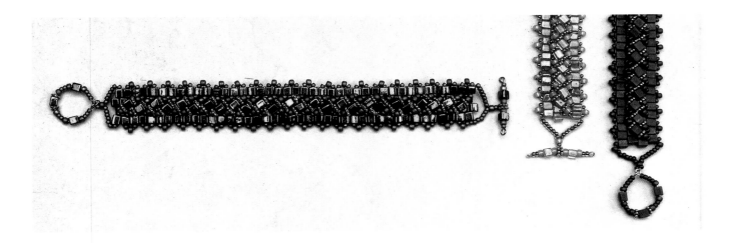

Embellished peyote bracelet

Cube beads made into a peyote band form the base of this bracelet. The top and sides are then embellished and a custom clasp unifies the design.

base

❶ Determine the length of the base by subtracting 1½ in. (3.8cm) for the clasp from the desired finished length of the bracelet. A 6-in. (15cm) peyote base has 41 square beads on each long edge.

❷ Thread a needle with a 2½-yd. (2.3m) length of Nymo or Fireline. String a stop bead 8 in. (20cm) from the end of the thread and go through the bead again in the same direction.

❸ String four square beads and work in even-count peyote (see "Basics," p. 4) until you reach the desired length.

embellishment

❶ Position the beadwork so the thread is coming out the top right square bead of the base. If your thread is getting short, weave it through the base, tie it off with half-hitch knots (see "Basics"), and start a new one. Pass the needle under the edge thread to the left (**photo a**) and back down through the end square bead (**photo b**).

❷ String a size 11º, an 8º, a spacer, a square bead, a spacer, an 8º, and an 11º.

❸ Pass through the fourth bottom edge square bead (**figure 1, a-b**) then go up the square bead to its left (**figure 1, b-c**).

❹ Repeat step 2 and pass through the next square bead along the top edge (**c-d**).

❺ Now skip a row. Go down through the next square bead to the left and the bead below it (**figure 2, a-b**). Go up through the next bead to its left and out the same edge bead (**figure 2, b-c**).

❻ Go down through the next square bead to the left (**figure 2, c-d**). Repeat step 2, skip a bead and go through the next square bottom edge bead to the left (**figure 2, d-e**).

❼ Continue adding top accent beads, following **figures 1** and **2**, until you reach the other end of the bracelet. Weave the thread through the beadwork, exiting the top left square bead.

❽ String an 11º, 8º, and 11º. Go down through the square bead to the right and through the next three beads diagonally. The needle will exit the bottom left bead (**figure 3, a-b**).

❾ String an 11º, 8º, and 11º. Go up through the square bead to the right and through the next three beads diagonally. The needle exits the next top square bead to the right (**figure 3, b-c**).

❿ Repeat steps 8-9 to the other end of the bracelet. Don't cut the thread.

clasp

❶ If you are using wire, cut two 2½-in. (6.4cm) pieces and make a loop (see "Basics") at one end of each wire.

❷ String two 11ºs, an 8º, a square, an 8º, two spacers, an 8º, a square, an 8º, and two 11ºs on one of the wires or an eye pin.

❸ Use chainnose pliers to bend the wire at a right angle as close to the last 11º as possible and in the same plane as the first loop (**photo c**). Trim the wire to ⅜ in. (1cm) and make the second loop.

❹ On the remaining eye pin or wire, string three to four 11ºs, an 8º, a square, an 8º, two 11ºs, an 8º, a spacer, a square, a spacer, an 8º, two 11ºs, an 8º, a square, an 8º, and three to four 11ºs.

❺ Form the wire into a circle around a cylindrical object, such as a marker (**photo d**).

❻ Slide the straight end of the wire through the loop. With chainnose pliers, make a slight bend in the wire where the loop and the wire cross (**photo e**).

❼ Place roundnose pliers in the bend and wrap the wire around the jaw of the pliers to form a loop (**photo f**). Trim the tail just above where the wire crosses itself and pull the loop closed with chainnose pliers (**photo g**).

❽ To attach the toggle ring to the base

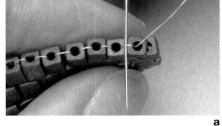

a

b

c

d

e

f

g

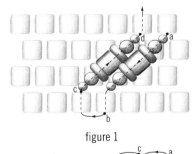

figure 1

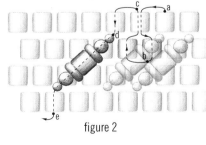

figure 2

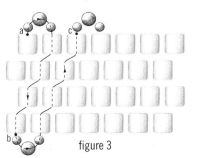

figure 3

h

i

j

materials

- 30g 4mm square beads
- 8g size 8º seed beads
- 6g size 11º seed beads
- **60** 4mm flat spacers, silver or gold
- **2** 2-in. (5cm) eye pins or 5 in. (13cm) 20-gauge wire, half-hard, silver or gold
- beading needles, #10 or 12
- Nymo D beading thread or Fireline fishing line, 6 lb. test
- beeswax or Thread Heaven for Nymo

Tools: chainnose and roundnose pliers, wire cutters

of the bracelet, string an 11º, 8º, and five to eight 11ºs on the needle and thread exiting the end bead on the base. String an 8º and an 11º and go through the loop on the toggle ring. String an 11º, and go back through the 8º. String the same number of 11ºs as you did above so the clasp is centered, then an 8º and an 11º. Go through the square end bead on the right-hand side (**photo h**).

9 Weave the thread across the base so it exits the same end bead as in step 8. Retrace the thread path a few times to secure the toggle ring. End the tail by weaving it through the base, tying a few half-hitch knots. Trim the tail.

10 Thread a needle on the tail at the unfinished end of the bracelet and string

eight 11ºs, an 8º, and an 11º. Attach the toggle bar to the base by wrapping the thread around its center (between the two spacers) four times (**photo i**).

11 Go back through the 11º and 8º (**photo j**) and snug up the thread. String eight 11ºs and go through the end bead on the right.

12 Retrace the thread path two or three times. Tie off and trim the tail. ●

– *Summer Melaas*

Square-stitch cuff

This versatile square-stitch bracelet can be customized to match just about any style. The base of 4mm cube beads works up quickly and easily accommodates a variety of decorative finishes. Try working with teardrop beads as shown in the black-and-tan bracelet, above, or put together a mix of multicolor size 8°s and small charms. For a completely different look, cover the base with malachite or other semi-precious stone chips.

bracelet base

❶ Thread a needle with a long piece of waxed Nymo or other thin, durable beading thread. String a stop bead and go through it again in the same direction, leaving an 8-in. (20cm) tail.

❷ Pick up four cube beads and slide them next to the stop bead. These beads comprise row 1. Pick up another cube bead and go through the last bead added in row 1 in the same direction as before. Continue through the bead just added to complete the first square stitch (see "Basics," p. 4 and **photo a**).

❸ Pick up another cube and square-stitch it to the next bead in the row

below. Continue adding rows of beads until your bracelet is the desired length (approximately 40-45 rows).

embellishment

❶ With the thread exiting a cube bead on the edge of the last row added, pick up enough decorative beads to cover one base row without any slack. Bring the thread over the base and back through the same row of cube beads (**photo b**).

❷ Before you string the second row of decorative beads, go through the next row of cube beads so the thread exits at the opposite edge of the row (**photo c**).

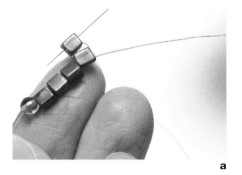

a

d

b

e

c

f

materials

- 25g 4mm cube beads
  (approx. 200 beads)
- 60g teardrop beads, a mix of teardrops
  and size 8° beads, or **2** 36-in. (.9m)
  strands small gemstone chips
- Nymo D beading thread to match
  bead colors
- beeswax or Thread Heaven
- beading needles, size #10 or
  twisted wire needles
- toggle or 2-strand slide clasp
- clear nail polish

end, bring the thread out at the center of the edge row, and sew on the other clasp half.

❷ Sew on the loop half of a toggle clasp in the same way. To attach the toggle end, string two or three cube beads to form a stem for the toggle bar. Go through the loop on the toggle and back through the stem (**photo f**). Go around the thread between cube beads and through the stem and toggle several times. Secure the thread in the beadwork and trim any remaining thread tails. ❍ – *Linda Gettings*

This may seem like an extra step, but it positions the surface beads to lie straight across each base row, not at an angle.

Pick up the decorative beads, bring them over the base, and go back through the second row of cube beads. Go through the next row of cube beads to position the thread for the third row of decorative beads.

❸ Continue embellishing cube bead rows with decorative beads until you've worked through every row of the base. For more fullness, add extra rows of decorative beads over the first layer. Then sew through the base, exiting through a cube bead at any corner of the bracelet.

❹ To cover the exposed thread and bead holes along the edge of the base,

string one or more decorative beads and go back through the same base row. String another decorative bead and return through the same row again. String another bead or two and go through the next base row. Continue adding beads in this manner until the holes on both edges of the base are covered (**photo d**).

❺ When you go through the last row of base beads for the last time, bring the thread out between the second and third beads in that row.

clasp

❶ To attach a slide clasp, sew through the loop (or loops) on one clasp half several times and secure the thread in the beadwork (**photo e**). Secure a new length of thread on the bracelet's other

Splash bracelet

Focal beads sewn over the profusion of looped fringe on this bracelet spread the fringe so it looks like someone has just jumped into water. You can vary the beads on the fringe by using more or smaller bugles and fewer or more seed beads as desired. Any way you make it, the abundance of fringe makes this bracelet a showstopper.

If you can, take the time to sand the ends of your bugle beads so they are smoother and less prone to cut your thread. Stitching the base goes faster with size 6º beads. But using size 8º beads results in more fringe.

making the base

❶ Thread a needle with 2 yd. (1.8m) of conditioned Nymo or Fireline. String a stop bead 4 in. (10cm) from the tail; sew through it again in the same direction.

❷ String enough 6º or 8º seed beads to go around your wrist with a ½-in. (1.3cm) gap. This is row 1.

❸ Stitch four rows of square stitch (see "Basics," p. 4) for a total of five rows.

❹ To end or add thread, sew back through the rows, tying half-hitch knots between beads (see "Basics"). When adding thread, start several rows back, make several half-hitch knots, and exit the last bead added.

adding fringe

Add fringe to the three center rows of the base. Don't add fringe to the outside rows because it will fold under the base.

❶ At the end of the fifth row of square stitch, turn and sew through the first bead on the fourth row (**photo a**).

❷ Pick up one 11º seed bead, a bugle bead, seven to ten seed beads, and a bugle bead. Sew back through the first seed bead and the next bead on the base row (**photo b**). Tighten the loop (**photo c**).

❸ Repeat step 2 to add loop fringe along the entire row. Go through the last bead.

❹ Turn as in step 1 and add loop fringe to the center row. Turn and add fringe to the next row.

a

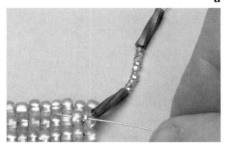

b

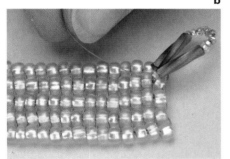

c

d

e

f

g

h

materials

- 15g size 6º or 8º seed beads
- hank size 11º seed beads
- 30g 10-12mm bugle beads
- 5-20mm focal bead
- 2-6 4-6mm accent beads or crystals
- Nymo D beading thread or Fireline fishing line, 6 lb. test
- beeswax or Thread Heaven for Nymo
- beading needles, #10 or 12

through the focal bead (**photo e**). Pick up the accent beads for the other side and sew into the center row (**photo f**), tightening the thread so the beads lie flat.

5 Turn and sew back through the center row. Pass back through the focal bead arrangement and into the center row again. Repeat for security.

making the clasp

1 Sew through the base to exit the end bead of the center row. Pick up enough beads to make a loop for the clasp bead. Make sure the bead fits snugly through the loop. Sew back into the center row (**photo g**). Turn and repeat the thread path several times to reinforce the loop.

2 Sew through an outer row of beads to the bracelet's other end or start a new thread. Exit the last bead on an outer row. Pick up five 6º or 8º seed beads, the clasp bead, and a seed bead. Skip the last bead and sew back through the clasp bead and two seed beads (**photo h**). Pick up three seed beads and sew into the other outside row. Repeat the thread path several times to reinforce the clasp bead. ◉

– Gayle Goddard

adding a focal bead arrangement

1 Lay your group of focal and accent beads over the fringe at the bracelet's center. Adjust the order and number of beads until you are satisfied.

2 Sew through the beads on an outside row of the base until you near the center. Sew through base beads to the center row.

3 Come out a bead on the center row two or three beads before the middle of

the row. Pick up the central focal bead and sew back into the center row far enough along that the bead lies flat and is centered (**photo d**). Before you tighten the stitch, arrange the fringe under the focal bead so that the same number falls to each side. Continue along the row and exit a bead far enough past the focal bead to fit the accent beads on one side of it.

4 String the accent beads and sew

Reversible bracelets

For something a little different, why not try some of the triangle beads that have become readily available in the past couple of years? Here's a fun way to take advantage of their unique shape: square stitch two or more colors together to make these unusual reversible bracelets.

These directions are for the two-color bracelet at the top of the page, but you can easily adapt the technique to make the other styles shown. The blue bracelet at left uses beads with slightly rounded edges, which gives the surface a ridged texture that's quite different from the smooth surface you

get using sharp-edged triangles. You can use three colors instead of two, mix matte and shiny beads, create stripes or geometric shapes, or work with triangles in other sizes. Just try to choose beads that are uniform in size to minimize distortion at the edges.

bracelet band

❶ To determine the finished length of your bracelet, measure your wrist and allow a little extra for ease. Subtract the clasp measurement (including any extra beads used to attach the clasp) to find the length of the beaded band.

❷ Working with a comfortable length

of conditioned thread, string a stop bead about 18 in. (45cm) from the thread's tail followed by 11 triangle beads in color A. (This number is given as a suggestion only; make the bracelet as wide as you'd like.)

❸ Work back across the row in square stitch (see "Basics," p. 4), adding one color B bead to each bead in row 1. Make sure to turn the beads so the new row and the previous one are always oriented with a flat edge next to a tip (**photo a**).

❹ Continue to work in square stitch until you're about eight rows short of the band length determined in step 1.

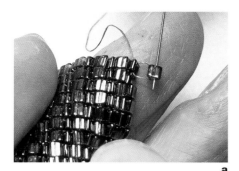

a

c

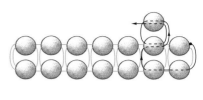

figure 1

b

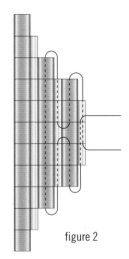

figure 2

materials—bracelet at top (p. 36)

- 10g each of 2 colors of size 10º or 11º triangle beads
- beading needles, #10 or 12
- Nymo B or Silamide beading thread
- beeswax or Thread Heaven for Nymo
- heavy-duty or reinforced beading thread
- reversible clasp such as S-hook with soldered jump ring, lobster claw, magnetic clasp, or slide clasp

Optional: toggle clasp with **2** 4mm round beads, **2** 2-3mm round beads, and **2** bead tips

adding a clasp

Here are a few options for finishing your bracelet:

❶ If you use a slide clasp, work to the full band length determined in step 1, above. Then sew through each of the clasp loops several times before securing the thread (**photo b,** top).

❷ Before attaching a hook or lobster claw clasp, taper the ends as follows: Decrease one stitch on each side for the next four rows or until three beads remain. (The number of decrease rows will vary based on the number of beads in your starting row.) To decrease in square stitch, backtrack through the next-to-last row, coming out the bead below where the new row will start. Go through the bead immediately above on the last row. Now begin the new row (**figure 1**).

Once you've stitched the last row,

bring the thread out on either side of the center bead. Go through the clasp loop and the center bead several times. Secure the thread in the beadwork. Finish the other end by threading the needle on the long tail left at the beginning of row 1. Taper this end to match and attach the second clasp half (**photo b,** second to top).

❸ To attach a magnetic clasp, taper the ends and secure the thread tails as in step 2. Anchor a short length of heavy-duty thread in the beadwork and exit one bead from the edge on the end row. String four beads, half the clasp, and another four beads. Go through the corresponding bead at the other end of the row. Go through the beads and clasp several times to reinforce the loop. Repeat on the other end of the bracelet (**photo b,** third from top).

❹ For a toggle clasp, taper the ends and secure the thread tails as before. Thread a needle with 12 in. (30cm) of

heavy-duty beading thread and weave it into the tapered rows as shown in **figure 2**. String a 4mm bead, a 2-3mm bead, and a bead tip onto both threads. Pick up an 11º bead on one thread and slide it into the bead tip (**photo c**). Slide the beads and bead tip close to the beadwork. Knot the threads around the seed bead using a surgeon's knot (see "Basics"). Glue the knot, trim the threads, and close the bead tip. Roll the bead tip's hook around the loop on a small toggle clasp (**photo b**, bottom). Repeat on the other end. ◉

– *Anne Nikolai Kloss*

Tubular herringbone bracelet

Make a snaky bracelet in a flash as you improve your herringbone skills. Even if you're new to this stitch, you'll find the project quick and enjoyable. Try it with size 5º triangle beads for a chunky feel or streamline it with 8ºs, as shown above. Make different versions and soon you'll be on a bracelet binge.

Work in herringbone to make one end of the bracelet. String the center focal beads, then stitch the second half. Add one clasp section, go back through the bracelet, and attach the other clasp.

bracelet

❶ Measure your wrist and determine the finished length of your bracelet. (This one is 8 in./20cm.) Subtract the length of your clasp, focal beads, spacers, and 6mm beads. This is how much herringbone you'll need for both sides. Divide this number in half for the length of each side. (These are 2½ in./ 6.4cm.)

❷ With 6 ft. (1.8m) of doubled thread, stitch a ladder of four triangle beads in alternating colors (**figure 1**). Leave a 12-in. (.3m) tail.

❸ Connect bead #4 to bead #1 (**photo a**). Strengthen by stitching through both beads several times.

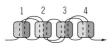

figure 1

4 Begin a herringbone stitch by holding the beads so the thread exits the top of bead #1. Pick up two triangle beads, keeping like colors stacked together. Go down bead #2 and up bead #3 (**photo b**).

5 Add two more beads, alternating the colors as before. Go down bead #4, up bead #1, and through the bead above it (**photo c**).

6 Repeat steps 4-5 until you reach your desired length. For 2½ in. of herringbone, stitch 23 rows of size 8º seed beads or 17 rows of 5ºs. Note that on the last stitch of each row, you always step up through two beads.

7 String a spacer, a small focal bead, a spacer, the large focal bead, a spacer, a small focal bead, and a spacer (**figure 2, a-b,** and **photo d**).

8 Pick up two triangle beads. Go back through the focal bead section, then go down the second triangle bead in the row (**figure 2, b-c**).

9 Work in herringbone as if the focal bead section isn't there. Go up the next triangle bead, through the focal bead section, and pick up two triangle beads (**figure 2, c-d**).

10 Go back through the focal bead section, down the last bead, and up the first bead in the row (**figure 2, d-e**).

11 Go through the focal bead section and up a triangle bead.

12 Resume picking up pairs of beads and stitching herringbone rows, making the second half of the bracelet to match the first half. Use ladder stitch to connect the last four beads.

a

b

c

d

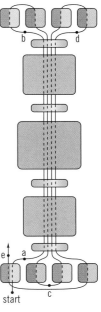

figure 2

materials

- **134** size 5º or **184** size 8º triangle beads
- **12** size 11º seed beads
- large focal bead
- **2** small focal beads
- **2** 6mm beads
- **6** 5-6mm spacers
- toggle clasp
- Fireline B fishing line or Nymo D beading thread
- beeswax or Thread Heaven for Nymo
- beading needles, #10 or 12

clasp

1 Go down the adjacent triangle bead and up the row's center. Add a spacer, a 6mm bead, six 11º seed beads, half the clasp, and three more 11ºs.

2 Go back through the first three 11ºs, then tighten to form a loop (**photo e**).

3 Go through the 6mm bead, the spacer, and a triangle bead. Go up the row's center then back through the 11ºs to reinforce the loop. Tie three half-hitch knots (see "Basics," p. 4), and dot with glue. When dry, weave in and cut the tail.

4 At the other end, thread a needle on the tail, then attach the remaining clasp section as before. ❍ – *Dottie Hoeschen*

Rickrack bracelet

Retro jewelry is popular again, so this bracelet, reminiscent of rickrack edging, should be at the top of your list of projects to make. After you make one for yourself, you may find you want to make them for all the women you know.

Keep the tension firm as you stitch to pull the beads into the triangular pattern and to make sure all the thread between beads is hidden.

❶ Thread a needle with 4 yd. (3.7m) of Silamide or Fireline. Using the thread doubled, pick up an accent color fire-polished bead (AC), a seed bead, an AC, a seed, a main-color fire-polished bead (MC), and a seed. Go through the first five of these beads again (**figure 1**). Your thread will be exiting an MC bead. As you tighten the thread, slide the beads toward the cut ends, but leave 18-in. (46cm) tails for attaching the clasp in step 11. Tighten the thread to bring the beads into a triangular shape.
❷ Pick up a seed bead, an AC, a seed, an MC, and a seed. Go through the MC in the previous triangle. Continue through the next four beads and exit the new MC (**figure 2**).
❸ Pick up a seed bead, an MC, a seed, an AC, and a seed. Go through the MC in the previous triangle. Continue through all these beads again, then exit the new MC (**figure 3**).
❹ Repeat step 2 (**figure 4**).
❺ Repeat step 2, but continue through all five new beads and the MC in the previous triangle (**figure 5, a-b**). Go through the five seed beads that form the inside circle, then go back through the MC in the previous triangle. Go through the new seed bead and exit the new MC (**figure 5, b-c**).
❻ Repeat step 2 (**figure 6**).
❼ Repeat step 3 (**figure 7**).

❽ Repeat step 3, but exit through the new AC (**figure 8, a-b**). Then go through the seed beads that form the inside circle and go back through the MC in the previous triangle. Continue through the new seed bead and exit the new MC (**figure 8, b-c**).
❾ Continue working in this pattern until your bracelet is about the same measurement as your wrist. (You'll add another inch/2.5cm when you attach the clasp.) Stop before you complete the last triangle. Pick up a seed bead, an AC, a seed, an AC, and a seed. Go through the MC from the previous triangle and the new beads again (**figure 9, a-b**). Continue through the inside circle of seed beads to

reinforce it and exit the MC bead from the previous triangle (**figure 9, b-c**).

10 Pick up 11 seed beads and go through the loop in one clasp half. Go through the third, second, and first seed beads strung in this step, making a loop of seed beads to attach the clasp (**figure 10**). Weave the thread back through the last few triangles to anchor the thread. Make several half-hitch knots (see "Basics," p. 4) between beads as you end the thread. Trim the tails.

11 Using the thread tails left in step 1, repeat step 10 to finish the other end of the bracelet. ● – *Anna Nehs*

materials
(7-in./18cm length)
- **42** 7 x 5mm fire-polished beads, main color (MC)
- **37** 7 x 5mm fire-polished beads, accent color (AC)
- Silamide beading thread or Fireline fishing line, 6 lb. test
- 5g size 11º Japanese seed beads
- beading needles, #10
- toggle clasp

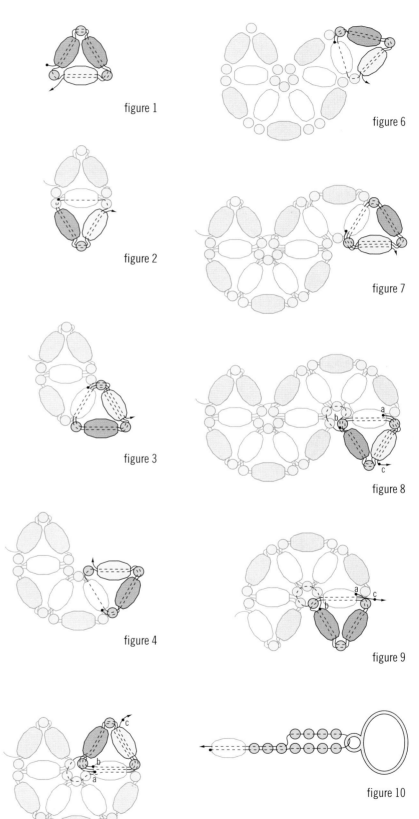

figure 1

figure 6

figure 2

figure 7

figure 3

figure 8

figure 4

figure 9

figure 5

figure 10

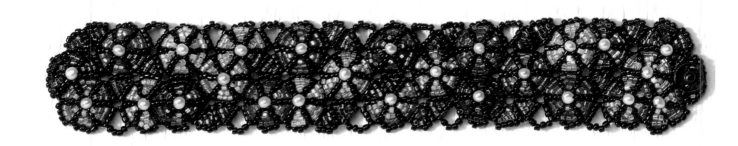

Flower garden bracelet

One of the great joys of beading is the way it opens one's eyes to inspiration. This bracelet, inspired by a triangle weave pouch by Tina Czuba, a beader from Illinois, is one example. Tina used bugle beads and seed beads to make her triangles, but seed beads alone accomplished the task just as well. You'll see that as you complete the base of the bracelet, the flower pattern becomes obvious. Japanese cylinder beads in a multitude of colors filled in the garden. The result is a floral bracelet with a stained-glass quality that blooms year-round.

When you run short on thread in this project, take off the needle and leave the tail unknotted. Also, leave a long unknotted tail when you start a new thread. Use these thread tails later to fill in the triangles. Knot them when the bracelet is finished.

form the triangle base

❶ Start with 2 yd. (1.8m) of thread. String 12 seed beads, leaving an 8-in. (20cm) tail. Pass through all 12 beads again and pull the circle tight. Tie a square knot (see "Basics," p. 4) with the tail and working thread. These beads

comprise your first "triangle," which will have four beads to a side.
❷ Pass through the next four beads again and pick up eight beads. Sew through the four beads just sewn through again and the first four beads just added (**figure 1, a-b**). Pick up eight more beads and go back through the last four beads sewn through and the first four beads added (**figure 1, b-end**).
❸ Continue adding triangles as in step 2 until the row is long enough to encircle your wrist with a 1-1½ in. (2.5-3.8cm) overlap for the snap. The bracelet will shrink about ½-¾ in. (1.2-2cm) as you fill in with Japanese cylinder beads.
❹ To start the second row, your needle should be exiting the last triangle of row 1 at **figure 2, point a**. Pick up eight beads and sew through the last four beads, continuing through all eight beads just added (**figure 2, a-b**). Pick up eight beads and sew back through the four beads just sewn through and the first four beads added (**figure 2, b-c**).
❺ Pick up eight beads and sew back through the four beads just sewn through and all eight beads just added (**figure 2, c-d**). Sew through the four

beads on the edge of the next triangle on the first row, pick up four beads, and sew back through the last four beads added, the four beads on the edge of the first row triangle and the four new beads (**figure 2, d-end**).
❻ Alternate a and b below to complete the second row:

6a. Pick up eight beads and sew through the last four beads sewn through. Sew through the eight new beads again (**figure 3, a-b**).

6b. Sew through the four beads on the edge of the next triangle on the first row. Pick up four beads and sew through the last four beads added in step 6a, through the edge of the triangle in the first row, and the four new beads again (**figure 3, b-end**).
❼ When you have completed the second row, there may be an extra triangle on the first row. If so, you will need to add three triangles to complete this end. Sew through the beads until your needle exits from the extra triangle at point A in **figure 2**. Repeat step 4 to reach point C in **figure 2**. Pick up four beads and sew through the near edge of the last triangle of row 2. Sew through the last four

figure 1

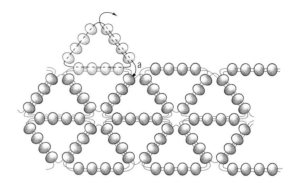

figure 2

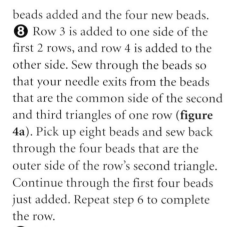

figure 3

figure 4

beads added and the four new beads.

8 Row 3 is added to one side of the first 2 rows, and row 4 is added to the other side. Sew through the beads so that your needle exits from the beads that are the common side of the second and third triangles of one row (**figure 4a**). Pick up eight beads and sew back through the four beads that are the outer side of the row's second triangle. Continue through the first four beads just added. Repeat step 6 to complete the row.

9 When you reach the other end of the bracelet, repeat step 8 to add a fourth row on the opposite edge.

fill in the flowers

To fill in the flowers, consider a circular set of six triangles a flower. Each triangular "petal" holds three rows of cylinder beads. The widest part of the triangle holds three beads, and one bead fits in the narrowest.

1 Come out the fourth bead on a side, string three cylinder beads, and go into the third bead on the opposite side. String two cylinder beads and go through the second bead on the first side. String one cylinder bead and go

a

b

through the first bead on the second side (**photo a**). Pull stitches taut to create a convex "petal" shape with the cylinder beads.

2 The triangles can be filled in infinite ways. Some blooms will be partial as in nature. You can shade the flowers with several tones of each color. Use green beads in some triangles for leaves, and leave some triangles empty as appropriate to the design.

3 Put a pearl or round bead in the center of each flower by sewing out one row into the center, picking up a pearl or round bead, and sewing into the row directly across (**photo b**).

4 When you have filled in your garden bracelet, sew the mates of a snap closure to each end of the bracelet.

materials

- 25g size 11º Japanese seed beads, black
- Japanese cylinder beads in assorted colors
- **25-30** 3mm pearls or round glass beads
- snap fastener
- Nymo D beading thread, black
- beeswax or Thread Heaven
- beading needles, #12

Knot the thread tails between the beads on a triangle wall and run them through a few more beads before trimming. ● – *Pam Nichols*

Diagonal lines bracelet

Cube beads are attractive and fun, but they can be a challenge to design with because they don't necessarily fall into place the way you'd think they would. In this bracelet, the cubes fall naturally into diagonal lines, and the pearl embellishments seem to grow out of the pattern.

Create a striped base by using two or more colors. For the embellishment, use 3-4mm fire-polished beads instead of the pearls if you wish.

base

1 Thread a needle with a 2-yd. (1.8m) length of Fireline. String two cube beads and leave a 10-in. (25cm) tail. Bring the needle up through the first bead in the same direction and down the second bead, to make a brick stitch ladder (**figure 1, a-b**). String a cube and go through the previous cube and back through the cube just strung (**figure 1, b-c**). String a cube and go through the previous cube (**figure 1, c-d**). The thread will exit the third bead.

2 String two cubes and go down through the second bead from the left on the previous row. Go up through the bead to the right and the second bead strung (**figure 2**).

3 String a cube and go down through the end bead of the previous row (**figure 3**).

4 Go up through the bead to the right and back through the last bead strung. String a cube and go down through the end bead (**figure 4**).

5 Go up through the cube to the right and the bead diagonally above it (**figure 5**).

6 Repeat steps 2-5, adding rows until the bracelet is the desired length less 1½ in. (3.8cm) for the clasp.

embellishment

1 At the end of the last row, bring the needle down through the bead to the right and each bead along the edge (**photo a**). When you reach the end of the band, turn it around and bring the needle down the next bead on the last row and up the third bead. Go down the last bead and reinforce the other edge as shown in **photo a**.

2 If your thread is getting short, weave it through the base, tie it off,

materials

- 16g 4mm cube beads or
  4g each of four colors
- **35-40** 4mm pearls or glass beads
- **2** 3-4mm accent beads for attaching
  the clasp
- 2g size 12º-15º seed beads
- Fireline fishing line, 6 lb. test
- beading needles, #10
- toggle clasp

a

b

c

d

figure 1

figure 2

figure 3

figure 4

figure 5

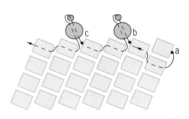

figure 6

and start a new thread. Position the needle so it exits the edge bead on the next-to-last row of the side you just reinforced (**figure 6, a-b**).

3 String a pearl and a seed bead. Go back through the pearl and through the next two edge beads (**figure 6, b-c**). Repeat until you reach the end of the base.

4 Weave the needle and thread through the base so it exits the edge bead on the next-to-last row on the opposite side of the bracelet. Repeat step 3.

clasp

1 Position the needle so it exits an edge bead on an end row. String six to eight seed beads, an accent bead, and five to seven seed beads. Pass through the loop on one of the toggle components and back through the seed bead before the accent bead, the accent bead, and the next seed bead (**photo b**).

2 String six to eight seed beads and sew through the other end cube bead (**photo c**). Bring the needle out the next cube bead and string four or five seed beads. Sew through the seed bead below the accent bead, the accent bead, and the seed bead loop (**photo d**).

3 Exit the seed bead below the accent bead. String four or five seed beads and go through the remaining cube bead.

4 Weave the thread through the base, tying half-hitch knots (see "Basics,"

p. 4) between a few beads to secure the thread. Trim the excess thread.

5 Thread a needle on the tail at the other end of the bracelet and repeat steps 1-4 to attach the other half of the clasp. ● – *Anne Nikolai Kloss*

Right-angle-weave pearl band

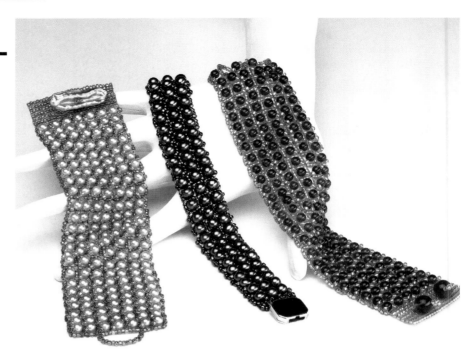

These beautiful pearl bracelets were designed by Karen Frankfeldt, a beading teacher in New Jersey. Karen is an excellent teacher and has a knack for getting across tricky techniques, including right-angle weave. According to Karen, success with right-angle weave lies in the mantra, "never, never go straight." When stitching right-angle weave, turn at every corner on the square, working alternately clockwise and counter-clockwise on each stitch.

These instructions make a bracelet three columns wide, as in the bracelet above, center. The bracelet can also be made wider as seen in the photo. Add the extra squares on the first row and continue from there. A box clasp is a fine alternative to a button-and-loop closure on the three-column bracelet. However, for a wider bracelet, use two button- or bead-and-loop closures, as in the bracelet above, right; or use an oblong bead or button, as in the bracelet above, left.

This is a wonderful project for honing your right-angle weave skills. For all its simplicity, it has an opulent, luxurious beauty and anyone who sees it will be impressed when you tell them it's your own handiwork.

bracelet base

When fitting this bracelet, remember it is a cuff and should fit comfortably around the wrist without sagging.

To add more thread while stitching, leave the thread tails unknotted until you've completed the embellishment.

Knots can block holes to beads you will need to sew through again. To secure a new thread, zigzag through the beadwork before positioning your needle to continue.

❶ Thread a needle with 2 yd. (1.8m) of Nymo and condition the thread (see "Basics," p. 4). Pick up 12 seed beads and tie them into a taut circle with a square knot (see "Basics,"), leaving a 6-in. (15cm) tail. Sew through the first six beads again (**figure 1**).

❷ Pick up nine beads and sew back through the last three beads and the first six beads added (**figure 2**).

❸ Pick up nine beads and sew back through the last three beads sewn through and all nine beads added.

❹ To begin the next row, pick up nine beads and sew back through the last three beads and the first three beads just added (**figure 3**).

❺ Pick up six beads and sew back through the bottom three beads of the previous row's middle square, the side of the second row's first square, and the six beads added. Sew through the bottom of the last square on the first row (**figure 4**).

❻ Pick up six beads. Sew through the side of the last square and the bottom of the first square again. Continue through all six beads just added (**figure 5**).

❼ Repeat steps 4-6 to add rows until the bracelet is long enough to fit around your wrist with ¾- to 1-in. (2-2.5cm) of ease.

embellishment

Pearls are only one embellishment option for this bracelet. You can choose any type of 4mm bead and even leave a pattern of squares unembellished. Add embellishment beads with a diagonal stitch across each square and a horizontal stitch down each column.

❶ Position your thread so you are at the outside corner of the last square added. Pick up a seed bead, a pearl, and a seed bead, and sew from the opposite corner out to the edge of the bracelet (**figure 6**).

figure 1
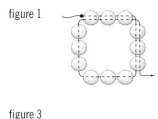

figure 2

figure 3
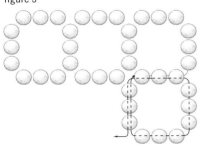

figure 4
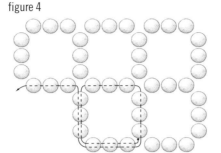

figure 5

figure 6
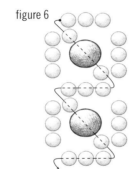

a

b

c

2 Add embellishment beads as in step one, zigzagging down the column.

3 At the other end, turn the bracelet over and sew through the base beads until you exit the top corner of the next square in the row. Embellish the middle column, maintaining the same stitch pattern as the first column.

4 Repeat step 3 for the last column.

end panels and closure

1 Sew through the beads to exit the three beads on the side of the corner square at the bracelet's end.

2 Continue through the three beads on the square's bottom side, pick up a seed bead, and sew through the bottom three beads on the middle square (**photo a**). Pick up another bead and sew through the last square's bottom three beads.

3 Sew two rows of square stitch (see "Basics") to this end row of beads.

4 Repeat steps 1-3 to add a panel at the other end of the bracelet. For the wide bracelets, add six rows of square stitch to one end and attach the buttons to it. Attach the loops directly onto the end row of base beads.

5 Sew a button at the center of one end panel. Reinforce the button attachment by sewing through it several times.

6 Add a loop of beads that fits snugly over the button to the bracelet's other end (**photo b**). Reinforce the loop by sewing through it a few times.

7 Alternatively, center one side of a box clasp on each panel. Sew through each clasp loop and pick up two seed beads. Skip the second bead and sew back through the first bead, the loop, and into the beadwork. Repeat for each clasp loop. Sew through the beads one more time for reinforcement (**photo c**).

materials

- **66-75** 4mm pearls or beads
- 20g size 11º Japanese seed beads
- **1** or **2** larger beads or buttons (7-10mm) for closure or 2-strand box clasp
- beading needles, #12
- Nymo D beading thread
- beeswax or Thread Heaven

8 Knot any thread ends with two or more half-hitch knots in the beadwork (see "Basics"). Glue the knots and sew through a few more beads before clipping the threads. ◗

– *design by Karen Frankfeldt, instructions by Carol Strauss*

Right-angle-weave cuff

The elegant shimmer of this cuff belies its simplicity. In less than two hours, you can whip up three rows of right-angle weave (see "Basics," p. 4). Use aurora borealis fire-polished glass beads to achieve the aqueous gleam.

1 Cut 2½ yd.(2.3m) of Gossamer Floss. String four fire-polished glass beads, alternating blue and green. Leave a 2½-ft. (76cm) tail and tie the beads into a snug circle with a square knot (see "Basics"). Glue the knot and pull it into a bead.

2 Thread a needle on the longer end and continue through a green, a blue, and a green bead on the circle. String a blue, a green, and a blue bead. Go back through the last green bead sewn through. Continue around the second stitch through a blue and a green bead. String a blue, a green, and a blue bead and sew back through the last green crystal on the previous stitch.

3 Continue adding three-bead groups until the chain almost reaches around your wrist with a ¼-in. (6mm) gap. String a blue bead and sew through the green bead at the other end of the chain. String a blue bead and sew through the last green bead in the chain to link the ends together (**photo a**).

4 To start the second row, sew through the next three beads of the connecting stitch, exiting a blue bead. String a green, a blue, and a green and sew through the blue bead you first exited (**photo b**).

5 Sew around this stitch through a green bead. String a blue and a green bead. Sew through the blue bead on the next stitch of the first row (**photo c**), the last green bead on the previous stitch of row 2, and the two beads you just added.

6 Sew through the next blue bead on row 1. String a green and a blue bead. Go through the green bead on the last stitch, the row 1 blue bead, and the green bead of the third stitch.

7 Repeat steps 5 and 6 to complete the row. The last stitch needs only one blue bead to join the first stitch.

8 Sew through the beads to the inside of the row. Tie two half-hitch knots (see "Basics") close to a bead and glue the knot. Pull the knot into the bead. After the glue dries, stretch out the tail and cut it so that the end pulls back into the bead.

9 Thread a needle on the long tail. Add a third row on the other side as in steps 4-8.

10 Thread a 12-in. (30cm) length of Gossamer Floss. Sew through a blue bead on the edge, leaving a 3-in. (7.6cm)

materials list
- **80** 6mm fire-polished beads, blue AB
- **60** 6mm fire-polished beads, green AB
- **40** 3mm fire-polished beads, silver AB
- twisted wire beading needle
- Gossamer Floss or elastic bead cord
- G-S Hypo Cement

tail. String a silver bead. Sew through the next blue bead. Repeat around the entire edge. When you have strung the last silver bead, knot the ends snugly with a surgeon's knot (see "Basics" and **photo d**) and glue. Sew the thread tails through a bead on each side and pull the knot into a bead. After the glue dries, trim the tails. Add silver beads to the opposite edge. ●
– Pam O'Connor